ACKNOWL

First and foremost, I must give honor and glory to my Lord and Savior, Jesus Christ. Thank you for giving me the talent of expression and for creating in me an honest demeanor by any means.

My mother would definitely come next. I love you so much, Shirley Jean Garrett, and I thank you with all of my heart and soul for raising a true lady with class and respect for herself and others.

My nephew, John "Johnny Rocket" Garrett, the best baseball player in the world ... I love you and miss you terribly. Thank you for being such a wonderful joy in my life.

I thank my only sibling, my older sister, Deneen "Wendy" Garrett for being my sister through it all. We may not have always gotten along but I am SO happy to be your little sister. I love you!!!

My other important family members: Reshema "Kissy" Young who is more like a sister than a cousin, her mother, my aunt, Gwen "Tee" Leeth, who is more of a second mother.

Dorothea "Suzy" Crawford who is more like a aunt than a cousin. Antonio "Deven" Crawford, my artist, more than a cousin, Uncle Ron Leeth, Henyo Crawford. Londa Wood-Rodgers ...

Thank you to my true friends: Marilyn "MoochGreedy" Nash, Shaton "The Diva" Andrews, Nicole Staley, Monique Macon to name a few ...

My business associates/friends: Reginald "Pharenhyt" Dockery, Al Venable, Vince Jackson ...

REST IN PEACE TO MY DOGG, RANDY "SAVAGE" COOKE !!! THIS IS FOR US, DOGG!!!

DEPENDING ON WHEN THIS BOOK DROPS, I ALSO MUST THANK THOSE WHO WERE INVOLVED IN MY BOOK SIGNING OR WHO WILL BE INVOLVED IN THE COMBINED BOOK SIGNING OF MY 1ST BOOK OF POETRY, *This Love Is Lyke A Four Letter Word*, AND THIS 2ND ONE.
I must thank the host of the event who also helped me get this event together, and I am so grateful. THANK U, the person I call my

Twin, Matthew LuckyLefty Sawyer; your expertise will and/or has made this event a success !!!

To the object of my affection, the collector of a sort, ... the reason I wrote this book: THANK U THANK U THANK U for being such a wonderful man ... I have never experienced this before. You are such an amazing person – so supportive, sweet, and all that other mushy and good stuff. Thank you and your parents for YOU!!!

SIDEBAR:
Genesis

These first three pieces have nothing to do with the object of my affection, but his support allowed me to write my most personal piece, *A Night in November in 2002*, and helped me to be able to share it without fears of any fault pointing fingers. I have become naked and unashamed from knowing him, and I thank him dearly.

The other two pieces are included because they too are personal, and it is my giving the middle finger to the devil and yelling, "you have me trapped and ashamed no more!"

Little Girl is about growing up without my father because he was murdered in November of 1980 when I was only five years old. The other two pieces are self-explanatory once you read them.

Little girl

WHO will cry for the little girl/the one with the pretty curls/ the one WHO lost her father's love/to a dumb maf*cka packin heat/trying to prove his worth/when only he destroyed her peace

PUNK maf*cka so selfishly/decided to take the masculine part of me/the part that was suppose to show me/how a man is suppose to treat me/a father's love/one I have never known/or do not remember/a precious and sacred commodity

NOT to discount my femininity/my mother/the greatest gift to me/but only reflecting/on something else important to me/a mother's love is eternal/a father's love may waver/or the feelings may not be known/if that father's existence is not felt

WHO will cry for me/when the world is trying to beat me down/confuse my mind into thinking that every smile is really turned upside down/WHO will mourn the lost/of a father's love that

WAS lost/snuffed out by pure evil and ignorance/leaving familial traces most evident

WHO will cry for the fatherless/while embracing a mother's job which is the toughest/WHO will cradle the heart/while the world constantly attempts to rip it apart/then wondering why hate rules the heart and mind of many

WHO will cry for YOU as you attempt to make a way out of the impossibilities believing in the possibilities and still rising about life's past negativities

Sort of like Death

11.13.03

March 1, 2003 is embedded in my soul like a cynical tattoo — images running in and out of my consciousness crawling through my psyche like a mental spider — each leg with a different image. Pain oozing from my pores like sweat from the hottest sauna and stretching my heart as if it was giving natural birth to a 15-pound baby.

Shots flew out and exploded through the outer surface of my face — bullet causing much internal damage before nestling itself between my chin and throat like a new chick snuggling under its mother's breast — pain from the bullet comforting me like an innocent prisoner locked inside his own cage full of rage attempting to push its way out of its new cell.

Now I am stuck with the images of the events and it feels sort of like Death — the shooting was my funeral, the pain my eulogy, the memory my eternal burial, sort of like Death yet slightly worse with thoughts penetrating my cognition reminding me of that mentally fatal night where innocent blood was shed for naught.

Sort of like Death causing an emotional miscarriage — blood exchanged with tears — tears with screams of despair while I feel trapped in a constant mental state of emotional purgatory.

A Night in November in 2002

It all started with an introduction, a cordial smile, and a handshake. He wanted to get to know me. I was nice but really not interested. He persisted; I resisted.

I sipping on a Moet split celebrating my bff's birthday, her 1 plus 25th. Through her own insistence, I let him buy me another split then I noticed it. Mouth dry, speech slirred, lightheaded, dizziness ... what is this? Not enough to be drunk it's crazy, I thunk.

Attempting to leave the club, I stumbled to my rental and then
Noticed him approaching me with 2 of his homies. One of them was dating my bff, so *exhale* I caught my breath and felt a comfort. "You cannot drive home. Slide over let me help you home." I complied knowing that I was with a friend of a friend and slide over for him to drive.

A gas station stop, red bull forced down my mouth, I felt ill vomiting up my entire meal what's the deal? "Let me help you; what you drink?" he asked, but I was unable to reply I felt a crazy new high; who is this guy.

Moments later I feel the familiar feel of clothes being removed and the unfamiliar tug of a trio wearing gloves ... no love. How did I get here? Isn't one of them my bff's dude? I feel sick room still spinning niggaz laughing, gasping, caressing, enjoying the sights, intrigued by my sexiness as they rip apart my intelligence attempting to say things making me think I am a participant and not a rape victim.

Years later, as my mind tries to erase this, I keep seeing that night looped in my memory wondering what I did wrong and how the fuck could this happen to me! Anger often fills my chest as I so many times check off my list of regrets. "shoulda did this. Shouldn't have done that," until my mind freezes on the images and fear ruled my existence knowing I would see them in the streets eventually.

A night in November in 2002, I was raped by three niggaz not just one or two. For so long, I hated the memory; didn't wanna think about it couldn't write it in a poem, but right now
I am
Releasing
It
All

And
Putting
My
Foot
On
satan's
neck,
while
yelling,
BITCH
U no longer have me trapped!!!

LET'S GET DOWN TO BUSINESS

YOU are about to enter a GROWN FOLK ZONE, so PLEASE, be prepared for anything. YOU will read pieces that are purely innocent showcasing the feelings inspired by a very special person to me, BUT YOU will also read explicit, erotic, and RAUNCHY pieces that inspired by this same man, may have you salivating.

DON'T JUDGE ME; JUST LOVE ME!!! LOL

Enjoy
And
PLEASE
ENTER
AT
YOUR
OWN
RISK !!!

THE CONTRACT

While I gotchu
I'm watchin' u ... meditate.
I can't wait won't hate or hesitate
To allow these words to sink in while we both
review this contract

CONTRACT? detailing this "ship of relations"
we're having sharing and exchanging our
most intimate PASSIONS
not just a continual conversation of our bodies
and souls blended into this SPIRITUAL hold
this contract holds rules and regulations of the
ultimate communication. I, let all my fears
and desires, hopes and dreams known open
and unashamed naked and embarrassment
free.
YOU, follow suit while we both agree to
change the rules as it fits our progression.
JEALOUSY? Nada. It is not allowed not
regulated in this ship of relations. We both
promise to keep it simply easy with only

complexities in how deep in conversation we engage thee.

As our bond is formed and we ease through the details of this contract detailing this ship of relations, it often seems crazy that things fall into place so smoothly. YOU, continue to DO YOU and date whomever you choose to. I, follow suit until we both decide when it's time to ... either put up and hook up or shut it down and go our separate ways.

This isn't a contract for the weak and weary. This contract is about STRENGTH. Some basic GROWN FOLK SHIT! As both parties consult personal counsel in attempts to provide our own ADENDUMS, the reality sinks in and comforts me. This isn't about being PLAYED. In essence, it is to PREVENT that. This contract details the ship of relations that we both freely agree to engage in.

Our INTENTIONS? Openly and honestly learn each other while still testing the waters in hopes to make sure that THIS ship of relations remain pure. Basic GROWN FOLK SHIT!

While I gotchu
I'm watchin' u … meditate.
I can't wait won't hate or hesitate
To allow these words to sink in while we both
review this contract.

With a twinkle in the eyes, south paws are
ready to make it official
He: "SO, are we agreed?"
Me: With a smile, wink, nod, handshake, kiss
on the cheek, signatures occupy above the
dotted line making this contract signed sealed
delivered and CONCRETE.

I'm "lovin;" you so much
You got my THROAT hurtin'

Slow ... moist ... soft ... gentle
Quick ... hot... hard... firm
Nibble... tongue flickering... love rising
...swaying
Curved to the right – a perfect shade of
melanin
TIP molded like a deadly mushroom ...making
me high off its evidence

Mmmm... I'm "lovin'" you so much you got my
THROAT hurtin'

Deep... long... thick...skin, slippery slick and
SMOOOOTH

My grind, steady wet heat driving all around
me
You make my head swirl lights bright but out
of sight as I, take you ever so deep
choke OOH SHIT. Mmmm ... tastes so
sweet
Left hand cupped under my head while my
whole mouth is giving you head and my left
hand controlling your sex and we both
moanin' of ecstasy cuz see,
I'm "lovin'" you so much
You got my THROAT hurtin'

Honey lemon halls... chips of ice
Tongue workin' overtime sliding down that
pole. Can't forget about YOUR twins

Ice melting between my slirps while my right
hand plays with your girth.
You're makin me high off your natural
perfumes of FREAK
Making my desires run deep as MY motion
goes DEEP and I accept every drop every
peep while you're in such a daze you look
sleep and down my throat your "love"
continues to creep, cuz shit Baby you got me

"lovin'" you so much my THROAT is hurtin' to
the touch, and I love it; thanks a bunch!

Sweat...heat... FIYAH... the desires won't let me just play for a second Mmmm ... I'm trying to take you to "heaven" while I'm searching your hidden treasures and hunting around for the anecdote

DAMN BABY!
I'm "lovin'" you so much
That's it's hurting my ENTIRE THROAT!!!

U got ME

U got me excited about waking up n the
morning.
Not needing the rooster to crow n the
morning I feel your soul in my soul n the
morning prompting me to start my morning.
U influence me to give HIM Praise n the
morning baptizing in HIS sun's rays n the
morning.
Encouraging me to be free in the morning.
Erasing my past shame as I once again get to
get life right again n the morning.

U got me matching up our names in the
morning.
Counting every letter's curve n the morning.
Hoping that ours is a perfect match n the
morning.

U got me picking out flowers in the morning
and I don't know a damn thing about flowers
n the morning.
I just know I want some pure fresh scented
beauty n the morning to match your
personality n the morning.

U got me crying tears of joy n the morning
happy to b in your world n the morning
awaiting your next lovely compliment n the
morning making me dreams dreams after
awaking from my dreams n the morning.

U got me wanting to make u breakfast n the
morning.
Serve it to u with a silver spoon on a silver
platter n the morning making sure you're
properly fed n the morning
in order for u to get the proper nourishments
n the morning.

U got me looking forward to the night n the
morning
n order to awaken the next day n the morning
looking forward to our next intimate moment
n the morning
where we can complement each of our day n
the morning.

U put a powerful move on me n the morning
not just our perfect sex n the morning
but with your entire human divinity n the
morning
making me call the Holy Trinity in the
morning.
making my blind eye see n the morning
watching your body leave n the morning
knowing your soul stays with me n the
morning.

I feel your power all day but having been
equally yoked in an unbreakable way causes
me with u to stay ... n the morning

Senses

I hear your heart beating in my dreams
As the blood pumps throughout my organs

I can smell your spirit and feel its non-
presence put a hole in my own soul

I feel your hands all over me
Although your absence is real
It still feels as if you're right next to me

I hear your light breathing in my ear
Whispering my name, Siamese Dear
I need not awaken to know you're really not
here
Cuz I can feel you gone even when you feel
so near

I taste your aura
Satisfying every taste bud
Making my mouth salivate
Licking my lips to the reality of your not being
here

I see your face on the inside of my eyelids
Tattooed on my retina viewed through my
pupils
Projected on my lens so every time I blink my
eyes a different picture transcends

I sense you all around me
Physically, emotionally, spiritually

I sense you in the morning while you are in
your own bed
I sense you in the afternoon while you are
also sensing me
I sense you at night when you are physically
with me
Our souls have united creating a mirror image
of inspiration
Physically sensing our separate and combined
creations
I don't know what has transpired but I know
my sensitivities to you keeps me empowered
energy on fire keeping my mind satisfied, full,
and tired

Finger power

Strumming my words with his fingers
Pulling out every moan built up inside
Controlling, with all my mite, my breathing
as my juices betray me by escaping
trying to learn his fingers' strokes
breath catching inside my throat
my mind is trying to grasp this truth

that this dude is digging out my past life's
youth

Strumming my words with his fingers
while making the middle one vibrate inside
I'm starting to lose my inhibitions
While my inner mind is screaming the entire
time
Resting in between his strokes and pokes
I realize that, over my body, he has taken
control

Strumming my words with his fingers
Pulling out every vowel and syllable
I'm trying to stifle my carnal soundtrack
Losing hope, I start to unleash it in stereo
Settling in for the long strong ride
Feeling his fingers glide and slide inside
While the nerves in my creamy dreamy
slippery thighs cause my legs to collide from
his digital vibes

Strumming my words with his fingers
Releasing all of my stress
I'm thinking about ice cream, cloudy dreams,
and long sleeves
OH SHIT I digress
my mind is at such a rest I EEAASSE to sleep
wrapped up in his arms

OUGNY AMN

I'm talkin' to my young man
The dude who showed me that a youngin can
be a GROWN MAN
He ain't with all that dumb shit
He's legit and doesn't mind showing me how
GROWN he can get

My young man
not to be confused by his age, MAN
holding the deepest conversation he's a
perfect assimilation of a poem and he loves to
take long walks by the water and
hold me around my waist makes me feel taller
and grabs my face and pulls me closer DAMN

I'm talkin' to my young man
not to be confused by his age, MAN
mind's sharp as a needle words be blazin'
powerful and important he's fuckin' amazin'

my young man
packin' like a criminal
sex game is imperial

Believe when I tell you, my young man's a winner

my young man
back strong as an ox
moves quick as a fox
last longer than Xbox
he knocks me out my socks

I'm talkin to my young man
Not to be confused by his age MAN
Taking me on sexual vacations
Stirring his jones like coffee mutha fuckin coffee
Poppin my cherry like I'm still a virGIN

My young man
12 years younger than my 35, MAN
His swag's better cuz he's in his prime, YEA
Makes me feel open, free, and alive

My young man

He gives vibes stronger than live wires
Every time he's around I get heated like a FIYAH

I'm talkin' to my young man

I know this tribute may seem kinda lame,
MAN
But I got this crazy 'like jones' and it's fun, I'm
sayin'
This is just another way to let you know,
DAMN

I ain't goin nowhere cuz you my young man

ANGEL ON EARTH

WHERE did u come from?
Perhaps u came str8 from
Heaven?
The Angels r mourning
Your soulful escape
Celebrating your
Presence and
Domination on
Earth

U have managed to
Infiltrate my psyche
Invade my ENTIRE body
And
Shoot an arrow
Of "in likeness"
Through my
Sentiment;

I didn't ask for it

But luckily

I was open
Enough
to not
let u pass
me up

WHERE did u come from?
Perhaps u left GOD's side
In order to be
By my side
Sensing there was a need
Of mine to be met

HOW many times
Did I almost let
A misunderstanding
Prevent me from receiving
A special Blessing?

HOW many times did u
Encourage me to be me
And with u
To express
myself fully?

WHICH side of Heaven
Do you truly belong?

U may have left GOD's side

But u have
Made my side
SO much stronger

WHERE did u come from?
Perhaps my dreams
And prayers
Finally came together
Made a connection
Created a bond
And even agreed upon
A beautiful language
To a powerful CONTRACT
Allowing me
To experience something
So sweet and genuine
LIKE
it is finally my time
To experience something
Kinda sorta like almost
DIVINE

WHERE did u come from?
Perhaps u r
THE BEAUTY REP
Of the Ultimate Creator
Exposing HIS
Perfect symmetry
Of life everlasting

When u
Allow
Yourself
To open up
Let go
Let GOD
Take control

WHERE did u come from?
Perhaps I missed the memo
Telling me that
There would b an
ANGEL ON EARTH
Perpetuating on EARTH
What would be
perpetuated
in HEAVEN
a preview
of a sort
of the pure
Supremity
Of Eternal
Blissfulness

HOW many times
Did I feel your aura
While being blinded
By your HALO
While attempting to

Not allow u
To access
My
Heart?

WHERE r u going?
Straight to the part of me
That usually tries to flee
When she feels her
Sentiment
Being invaded by a
Beautiful
Stranger

WHERE r u going?
To a place in me
That allows me
To MAN UP
And be free
Free enough
To open up
Enough to
Get to know
The ENTIRE u

WHERE r u going?
To a place
Where I am able to
Learn your name

In every language
Starting with your past
Names
And ending with the ones
Uttered in non shame

MY ANGEL
ON
EARTH
The one
who
I
appreciate
the most
and
have dedicated
an entire book

WHERE did u come from?
Perhaps u came str8 from
Heaven?
The Angels r mourning
Your soulful escape
Celebrating your
Presence and
Domination on
Earth
And luckily
I didn't spoil

Your search
Through my SENSES
In order to
Help me
Experience
ULTIMATE
AND
DIVINE
BLISS

Beauty Rep

Beauty has a representative
and that person is you
You exemplify beauty
to its deepest roots.
I am beyond fascinated
by everything you do
Watching you watch me

sends tingles
        throughout my entire body.

GOD created a masterpiece
        When HE designed you
Perfectly sculpting you out
        From your face to your shape
        To your personality and creativity

Beauty has a representative
        And that person is you
There's something about your beauty
        That makes ME wanna WOE you
From your sexy eyes to those delectable lips
        To the way you stare at me and the way
we kiss

Beauty has a representative
        And that person is you
You exude beauty
        With everything you do
From the way your presence
affects the multitude
        To the way your words
        are fed to me
        like intellectual food

Beauty has a representative
        and that person is you

your energy causes
     my heart to skip
     a beat or 2
from the manipulation of your humor
to the secret seductiveness of your demeanor
beauty's representative has taken on a whole
new meaning

beauty has a representative
     and that person is you
defined as a quality
     that pleases or delights
     the senses or mind
     I find your quality
     quite anointed and divine

beauty has a representative
     and that person is you
You exemplify beauty
     to its deepest roots.
I am beyond fascinated
     by everything you do
Watching you watch me
     sends tingles
          throughout my entire body.
I ask that your beauty
     meshes with my beauty
     And we create one: UNITY

Do U

Take a look @ me

do u like what u c

I am your destiny

completing your thoughts and sentences

i leave your mind with a pleasant sense

showing u My loyalty

disbelieving all the he say and shes

accepting your style or lack there of

i make it my business to still give u my "love"

do u like what u c

i AM the real thing

no need to check your enemies

that will only offend me

Do U

Know what TREU'TH is

I'd rather think U haven't a clue

So before THIS gets out of hand

I promise to always

"Love" U

Halo

Radiance
Aura
Ring of LIGHT
Glory
Defined as a circular band of colored LIGHT
around a LIGHT source

Illuminated
Honored
Spiritual
Stellar
Redefined as an ignited crown surrounding a
LIGHT SOURCE of distinction and intrigue

I see you in my space
The air that I breathe
I swallow your poetic scents
Trying to control my heart
Help it ease

Past pain automatically erased
No need to fake an escape
You have created a fresh sense in me
Like an excited extra exhale
Body relaxed mind stress free
I'm constantly feeling the great energy in me

Honoring your spirit
Respecting your inner beauty
Celebrating our every meeting
Ever appreciating how you handle me
Taking control of me
But always listening to me
Really listening to me
Accepting the crooked letter of me

Radiance
Aura
Ring of LIGHT
Glory
Feeling the sun's constant rays as we pass the
day
Frolicking in life's wonder
I wonder how you broke the mold
How you pushed through life's life
Unscathed and completely whole

Illuminated
Honored
Spiritual
Stellar
Few things that I cherish about you
Happy to be able to be open with you
Almost missing missing missing out on you
Stubborn old hurt ways almost caused
our ship of relations to stray

Feeling your LIGHT
your shine
your power
your INTENSITY
has allowed a freeing in me

allowing you to break through my hard outer
core
into the best part being my nucleus

Feeling awakened, calm, and free
Being with you has allowed me to be ME
ALL OF ME
Finding comfort in my addiction to you
Breaking all the rules
Justified by your strength

Of my past ills and silliness
I repent

Radiance
Aura
Ring of LIGHT
Glory
Defined as a circular band of colored LIGHT
around a LIGHT source

Illuminated
Honored
Spiritual
Stellar
Redefined as an ignited crown surrounding a
LIGHT SOURCE of distinction and intrigue

I feel it

I see it
I breath it
I hear it
I've touched it
It's your HALO
The crown has you surrounded
Keeping you well-grounded
Illuminating your wisdom and Spirit
Your infinite eternal power and I want to
forever be in it

I WAS INSPIRED NOT TO WRITE ABOUT YOU

I am sitting here deciding decisions based on
misunderstandings
Of desires lost

Something HAS been lost
Although my smile remains bright calm cool
collected
My mind screams FUCK IT! I am better than
that
No longer will you experience the true
essence of me
That undeniable wall has reappeared to
protect me
As I peck these words out from my bosom's
nucleus
I realize that I was inspired NOT to write
about you

Something new has changed into something
blue and it has caused a rip in something that
seemed so innocent fresh and pure
Although my smile still shines like an Arizona
sunrise
My heart has created an ice sculpture where
my affection USED to be
I am sitting here playing with these words
rearranging these verbs and I realize that for
the first time since we met, I am inspired NOT
to write about you

Sometimes, it is not realized that, as a
woman, we too can compartmentalize our
emotions once some bullshit has gone down

Although our smile still rules our outer
appearance
Our insides are screaming you shouldn't have
done this
You done fucked it up now don't you see
I am sitting here replaying our conversation
on the mental screen of my mind and really
for the first damn time,
I am inspired NOT to write about you

You may wonder where now does that leave
us
I won't trip
I won't completely dip
I won't fuss but please know that I am truly
disgusted
Although my smile rises and widens across my
facial horizon and my eyes still dazzle and
twinkle like the stars
On my skin, reality sinks its sharp bitter teeth
and gnaws on my faculties numbing me of
your feelings
I am sitting here writing the ending to this
wonderful like story, and I realize that I am
inspired NOT to write about you

GONE
(it is what it is)

You've put another move on me
A move that no longer
Controls the soul in me
I'm starting to DRIFT AWAY
Feeling my mood
Turn from light to gray
HEAVEN only knows your intent
I admit
This shit
Is turning me into a BITCH

Putting another clip in the Glock
And unlocks ...
Feeling the PASSION leave from me
TIMBER!!!
Like a fallen tree

It's easier for me to flee
Than to deal
With these feelings in me
I'd rather walk away now
Than later drown

In my sorrows

CHOMP!!!
Another one bites the dust
I refuse to cuss
Or to fuss
But I'm holding down
The white flag and towel
Fuck throwing it in
I'd rather burn the bitch, NOW

You can't fuck with THE TREU'TH
Not suffering any repercussions
I deserve BETTER than that, TRUST

Forever dreaming a fairy tale
I prevail
As I slither away unharmed
And unscathed
Bathing in my own victory

CONFUSION?
Never even asked for you
To pursue
But there you went
And here I go
Going
Going
GONE ...

Sometimes, it really is
ONLY
About fucking
And now
I'm done
So
FUCK IT!!!

Thank you
For the INSPIRATION though

WINK

LIGHT

Ear burning
from the venom spoken.

how could my left eye
or perhaps
my 3rd
not have seen

that the reality
was never genuine.

Seeing U
for this new U
I realize the shit
may be true.

Eye stinging
from reading
all the messages
giving me
insight
I never asked for.

TRUTH
comes to
TREU'TH
now my feelings
r on mute.

3rd eye

buzzing

popping
and

rolling

not wanting to process
the information
but noticing

It makes sense.

And when
that was said
and that
was done
and
especially
when u were
touched there?!

Yea there!!

Same routine
for everyone.

not being mean
just being real
so

either

bounce
or

step

real

light

light

light ...
Just to know the ENTIRE you

I wanna learn your name in every language
Spelling every vowel and consonant for
emphasis
Inhale any accent marks to start
While ripping the sounds apart

I wanna learn your name in every language
From your past life to your future
I plan on taking my time
Just to know the ENTIRE you

I wanna walk inside your soul
And Stroll through your mind
Reading your thoughts
While reaching your vocal cords

I wanna browse past your heart

And memorize its rhythm

I wanna sit behind your eyes
Watching how you interpret the world

I wanna watch your blood flow
Recognizing how deep or how shallow it goes
Ever mindful of which ideology takes control
I plan on taking my time learning you
Just to know the ENTIRE you

I wanna swim in your speech
Rolling around while you speak
Learning which words you over-pronounce
Or which ones you under-enunciate

I wanna back-stroke through your syllables
Concentrating on your spoken mentals
Patiently taking my time NOT to miss SHIT
Cause THIS shit is deep

I wanna dream your dreams FOR YOU
Making sure you reach them too
Learning all your excitement
And fears
Erasing any hidden tears

I plan on remaining serious
Inquisitive and curious

Asking all the questions I deem important
While listening to everything you DON'T say
Making sure I watch what you DO say
in order to truly know you in every possible
way

I promise to pay special attention
As not to miss a thing
and plan on taking my time
To get to know what I plan to make MINE

Don't want to scare you or wear you out
All this I will do
just to know the ENTIRE you

I am NOT a COUGAR

COUGAR: see Mountain Lion.
MOUNTAIN LION: A large WILD cat of mountainous regions of the Western Hemisphere, having an unmarked tawny body.
WILD: uncivilized, savage; not domesticated or cultivated
WILD: unruly; full of uncontrolled emotion; erratic
UNMARKED: the opposite of: having a distinguishing mark; clearly defined; noticeable;
UNMARKED: the opposite of: outstanding; purpose; distinguished; striking; remarkable
COUGAR:A capable stalk-and-ambush predator, the cougar pursues a wide variety of prey or
URBANLY defined as an older woman who frequents clubs in order to score with a much younger man.
SCORE: a notch or incision; to game in a contest; to orchestrate or manipulate as in her intent to prey on younger men instead of desire of ONE younger man

FUCK THAT! If you wanna call me a cat call me a Black Panther.

PANTHER: powerful, intelligent, exotic, wild ...
(smirk)
WILD: intense, passionate; concentrated,
consuming; profound, sharp, strong
A Black Panther with a ten-point program of
empowerment not a Cougar whose goal is to
score and prey without the type of wild
tendencies that roams and strays

I am NOT a COUGAR! I do not search to seize
a man whose age is far under me, BUT I have
found one whose maturity far exceeds the
men whose company in my past I've
achieved.

As a matter of fact, don't even call me a cat.
CAT: animal; catcher of rats and mice
CAT: hunters of vermin and household pests

BULLSHIT! If u wanna call me a name call me
a beautiful woman.
WOMAN: adult female human being
WOMAN: wife; lover; sweetheart
WOMAN: aunt, daughter, mother, sister,
matron, grandmother, GOD mother
Also known as a vessel for life, creation,
Venus; queen, perfect helpmeet
With femininity and sex appeal that makes a
man drool just by the way she simply moves

As a matter fact, a woman is the other side of GOD. The sensitive side that influenced HIM to turn HIMSELF into HIMSELF as HIS Son to die for...

A woman ...

I am NOT a COUGAR, so please, next time get it right. My smooth and holistic style with lady-like charm and sophistication has just stepped into the ring, taken off the gloves, standing in my corner while you REGAIN your composure ready for the bell to ring for this knock out drag out Heavyweight match, but actually I already WON the title because I am a WOMAN; we carry the purse, and we ALWAYS win!

In *Cursive*

His tongue
spells my name out
in *cursive*

My unlimited
oceans
is his ink

He uses his tongue
as a pen
dipping it
into my sweet well
with each letter
his tongue speaks

He's a master
@ pleasing me
Dotting every I

and
crossing every T

He wears my
creemee
soft
thick
thighs
as his guide
while using his fingers
to bring me deeper
into his
spelling drills

His face
is a Master Spy.

Finding ALL
my hidden
secrets

His tongue
spells
my name
in *cursive*
and
he's even writing my name
in Japanese and German

When he's finished on one side
he flips me over
like the end
of a letter
on its first page
While spelling out
an arrow
and
the words
TURN PAPER OVER
from my thighs
to my side
from my side
to my back
Gently
firmly
arching up
my ass
to finish the task

Face drowning
in my
sensual notebook
my fountain
of
TREU'TH
while I create
my own soundtrack

of ecstasy
while he is completely
and
unselfishly
pleasing me

No need
to purchase another pen
this 1 is most definitely gettin it in!

His tongue
spells
my name
in cursive

tracing
my goals

in cursive

spelling out
his motives

in cursive

while I'm losing
my mind

in stereo

while I'm losing
my mind

in his
FINEPRINT!!!

Make Me

Make me
beg u
to stop

As I hear
and
feel
my pussy
pop
I notice
u getting
stronger
and
harder
and
in my mind
I'm praying
please
don't
stop

I got a
drive
that's sick
always ready
for it
never tire
of it
I'm an animal
of a sort;
an exotic
fat
cat
of a sort
Maybe a cougar (laugh)
definitely a panther
yearning for her Seabiscuit (laugh)

make me
make me
make me

beg u

to stop
I'm daring u
to challenge me
battle with me
put yourself

in charge
of the purr
in me
Challenge yourself
to sexually
attempt
to
break me
Make me
say
every name
you've ever claimed
causing my voice
to go hoarse
my hair
to drown
from our sweat
My lips
to swell up
from our serious

kissing

licking

sucking

fucking

make me
beg u
to stop
with my arms
push us
apart
the river overflowing
now starts
as i write
these words
and
read these words
u need
to know
how soaked
I am
just
from the thought of u
the memory of u
the anticipation
of my next time with u

Just hear my cry
feel my plea

beg u
to stop !

ooh Daddy

please
make
me!
Thank U, SAM

I want to thank
all the SAMs
from my past.

Thank u
for cheating
on me

Thank u
for not
supporting me

Thank u for,
had I ever been pregnant,
wanting to abort me

Thank u
to all
my SAMs
my sorry ass man(s)

the ones
who never had

my best interest

the ones
who were
too afraid
to show
their feelings.

I thank u
for being u
n order for me
to see TREU'TH.

Truth of
a real man
who exudes
the very
opposite
of
u.

Cuz without u,

I would never
c him

so SAMs
I truly thank u

never stop
being
who
in essence
is
u.

UPGRADE

Let me upgrade u
make plans to fly u to an exotic land while
making love on black sand
 Bypassing Disney Land

I'm trying to make u my man.

Let me upgrade u
take u from Ponderosa to Ruth's Chris House
ordering meals from the menu: top notch.

Let me upgrade u

leave Northland for the kids travel across 14
to Somerset for a fly new wardrobe.

Fuck Miller Lite let's sip on Moscato
Left pinky up if u can't afford it I got u.

Let me upgrade u

spa and play dates with breakfast in bed
accessing our financial portfolios
 as oppose to perusing youtube

let me upgrade u

with deep conversations about fears and
insecurities
and not just about sex and how u wanna do
it, Gee.

A make love conversation not just simply
tawkin bout fuckin'.

Let me upgrade u

not as yo Suga Mama
but as a grown woman
who can hold u down while u rise up
surpassing your own potential.
Upgrade u
won't say I made u
just wanna help U shape
who U r trying to be.
I'd never try to change u
just offer my grown woman maturity.

Let me upgrade u

help u move mountains beyond your wildest
dreams and cream
from the feeling of major success and
accomplishments

As time progress
u will c
that being upgraded by ME
will crown u a true KING

WHY SHOULD I CARE

I c
the twinkle
n your eyes

and

I c
how u
were surprised

by my
sudden
change
of
heart

ahem,
let me
explain
for starters

i found
a
precious gem
n him
and
wanted
to keep him
for myself

how selfish

when he belongs
to the craft
anyone else
would laugh
but
I
understand

u can't b a man
while I'm
STILL
holding
your hand

constantly
looking over
your shoulder
wondering if I
would let u
crawl ...

crawl

so u could
walk

walk
so u could
run

run so u could
fly

fly
n order to soar
high
n the sky

why should I care

i care
because
I've been there
and realize
it aint fair
to keep u
chained
deep
down
there
not allowing
your wings
to spread

spread wide

to spread
high

spreading high
to touch
beyond the sky

for

your

own

slice

of

HEAVEN's

pie

VISIONS

Having precious visions of my next decisions

still on top of my original mission

sidetracked for a smidgen?

NEVER

I maintain

my gift

of

wisdom.

Always on top

of my game

even through

my pain

and

disdain

but

my personality

remains the same

ever smiling

with

my lips,

eyes,

and

entire heart

nothing

and

no one

can tear

THAT apart.

Designed to survive

and

built to last

moving forward

forgiving

while

never

forgetting

my past

something about me

could never

hate

so I always

with

honesty

and

forgiveness

participate

never want

to stunt

my growth

I allow knowledge

to forever

take hold.

Remembering

my

visions

disregarding

the ignorance

I exhale

while

still

I

rise

I

RISE!

Closure (2010)

Didn't want it
Didn't ask for it
Didn't really seek it
But I got it
Closure

Not gonna fight it
Not sure if I like it
Not cool how u went about it
But I got it
Closure

Nothing left to do
Nothing else to say
Nothing lost between us 2
But I got it

Closure

Should've seen it coming
Should've warned my heart
Should've ran before it started
But I got it
Closure

Thank you for the pain
Thank you for the inspiration
Thank you for NOT keeping it fully real
But I got it
Closure

Wish things were different
Wish this pain would end
Wish I could do it again (cuz I wouldn't)
But I got it
Closure

Too GODly to hate
Too beautiful to be jaded
Too gifted not to use this
But I got it
Closure

I am love
I am peace
I am Treu'th

And this always prevails
And I always win
So although I wanted more
And got less
I got something much better
Closure

SIGH

This was my best project YET, and I pray that you enjoyed it and was inspired, motivated and even Blessed ...

THANK U for your continual support of my PASSION !!!

Love
Soltreu

Thank you crystal
Coleman for your

Presence and advice

Made in the USA
Charleston, SC
13 June 2010